CONTENTS

FOREWORD

The real trouble with living is that we die without ever getting to know why we did any of it. Sometimes, we find ourselves asking "why?" knowing we won't get an answer. But more often, we avoid that question and move. We trade reflection for activity as we understand reflection can only lead to an unanswered question. So we act. We do. We say. We move. And these become such a habit that every once in a while we catch ourselves in the middle of all our movement—all our avoiding, really—and between the series of anxieties we make of life, we think, "What the fuck am I doing?"

Enter Heather June Gibbons, an emerging voice in American poetry who I expect will be just as feared as any other voice that insists on the truth. In her first book, *Her Mouth as Souvenir*, Gibbons doesn't just admit to these anxieties of life. She glories in them and goes as far as claiming that living itself can only be valuable when we are honest about our mindless activity, when we admit to ourselves that we have no idea what we're doing or why, and that it doesn't matter because we're going to keep on keeping on anyway. The very first independent clause of this volume is quite literally, "My project is plain persistence," from a poem aptly titled, "Smell the Moxie."

Of course, our theories, philosophies, and ideologies do not make for good poetry. My interpretation of this book has very little to do with my desire to read it over and again, or my passion for sharing it with you. My attraction to

Gibbons's poetry is rooted in her ability to organize life's chaos without dulling its energy. Her mode is mainly free verse with rhythms and sounds that pulse forward under a kind of musical pressure, pushing us from the title to the last line, leaving us with the overwhelming feeling we have at the end of a long day. In a short amount of space, Gibbons uses the lyric to do what we would do to ourselves anyway. She means to wear us out. And while the images—she is a poet of the image as well as of sound—are stark without being surreal, her quick and skillful grab at what seems quite disparate in a single poem feels both absurdist and surrealist. This is from "Exploded View":

> We stagger around with the sound off,
> the sky a pale bruise, burst capillaries in our cheeks
> recording force the way a horizontal cross-section reveals
> growth rings in a tree. We are told no one was harmed
>
> in the making-of, the shattered window mere sugar glass,
> but I felt the floor quake, I saw a woman's skin lit
> like a lamp. I remember driving under a blue bridge.

And then later in the same poem, as if to make sure we understand she's been holding our hand the whole time in something we feared but understood, "What I am showing you is the exploded view."

Heather June Gibbons is not a confessional poet, but like all great poets, she understands there is no such thing as a poem that isn't autobiographical. The life of the mind is a life lived. Her speaker has at her access every image surrounding any single observation and all of the history that could lead to

that observation. If the world is a restless one, even that
restlessness is inherited:

> My people walked over mountains and buried children
>   on the trail
>   for a prophet who led them to a lake of salt.
> Now they polish the temple in their secret clothes, for
>   my people
>   are luminous. Though I can't see them, they
>   whisper, *you owe us.*

We are stuck journeying—toiling, you might say, in the
religious sense—until we can fix our eyes on someone who
will journey with us. The frustrations of the first part of this
book take a detour for the frustrations caused by Eros in the
second part. As if calling out to those ancestors buried "on
the trail," Gibbons's speaker seems to pray in "Crossing," "I
do not name, nor do I whisper after dark. / In not naming, I
call out / in hopes of being called." And in one of several
poems titled "Sore Song," she addresses Eros directly and
damningly until conceding, "For you, we do the singing."

And don't we prefer that little mischievous god named
Eros to the one to whom we imagine our parents and
grandparents prayed, to whom they would have us pray?
Aren't our prayers to Eros the most rapturous ones we utter?
For instance, in another one of these "Sore Song" poems
Gibbons writes:

> I need your thumbprint on me in glitter or in ash.

> I looked for you in bulk bins of star anise,
> in the creases of bus seats, in strange twangs

and interstate clovers, mistook you for other
pangs and baubles, and lay awhile panting

in your shadow, laid wait in stairwells
and in the body's many clefts, whispered

for you, parched....

Progression in this book, like progression in life, moves us
forward in time but not in wisdom. We still don't know why
or what the fuck, but we understand loss as a result of gain.
And the poems remain strong and wide-eyed to the end as
they turn from exclamation in the first section to prayer in
the second and to elegiac in the third. Elegy itself has no
bounds as the speaker commemorates all she once felt
badgered by—love, work, the city, unending breath:

We, too, used to work in shifts.
We want something scalable, less whirling.
The meds keep us even, but we miss desire.
The dream was so bad it woke me.
I was holding myself.
Like the stabbing realization of loss, anticipated.

Or, as Gibbons herself says in the wild ride of the poem "The
Green Rose Up":

So, we left the city, we left our clothes.
We lined up at the agency and spoke
only of our strengths and not of the law
that keeps us upright in the Rotor ride,

ironed to a curve. When we say we want
to live in the moment, what we mean is
we want not to want an impossible future.
To be conscious of every breath
is to be unable to think of anything else,
which is to say, happier.

I am trying to say that I love this book and the way it cries
out in well-crafted poems that aren't under the impression
that craft has anything to do with boredom. *Her Mouth as
Souvenir* is a declarative wonder, a testament to our need to
go and go on.

Jericho Brown
Atlanta, Georgia

I

SMELL THE MOXIE

My project is plain persistence, self as spatula
scraping self as burned crud off skillet, pretend
research in a field of forget-me-nots sprayed
with real pesticides, grief that never gets past

bargaining, the whole *what if* and *if only*,
elaborate mazes out of wet cardboard, a little
cologne for the armpits, we're talking real
Band-Aid solutions here, a jerry-rigged screen

door on a sagging front porch where a man
with a shotgun across his knees is sleeping,
an outboard motor that starts up about every
umpteenth yank, but only when you choke it.

I have this habit of breaking keys off in locks,
drawer knobs come off in my hands, slobber
dries on my thighs, when I say *doing okay*
I mean an ongoing white-knuckling, when I ask

how you are, I hear furnace, then praxis, think
wax, expats, and other kinds of justice, tell you
can't, have to walk my hair and wash the dog,
key my own car then drive it through a wall.

Pennies over my eyes and still this throb
in my trousers. Not a pretty place. Left
to my own devices, I play until they break.
I keep turning this roll of invisible tape

hoping to catch an edge I can peel from.
Who wants to see my discursive knees?
Cordon the fire lane, adjust the thermostat,
squeeze out the very last dab of paste.

When I say *take a stab*, I mean get a grip,
meaning grasp, meaning straws.

EXPLODED VIEW

Etched into each fallen leaf is a diagram of a bare tree.
Things come with their own directions. They tell us
what we are about to see will likely appear senseless.
We say we want no part in it, but no one hears us

fall in the woods. We stagger around with the sound off,
the sky a pale bruise, burst capillaries in our cheeks
recording force the way a horizontal cross-section reveals
growth rings in a tree. We are told no one was harmed

in the making-of, the shattered window mere sugar glass,
but I felt the floor quake, I saw a woman's skin lit
like a lamp. I remember driving under a blue bridge.
Later, I will produce a histogram of the image to better

manipulate the colors. A somewhat random sample
of a hundred observations from the normal distribution,
shards of ice angled on the creek breaking against each other.
We hadn't seen anything of this magnitude before,

except for the time the hounds found the wounded elk.
Blood in the snow, a red telephone and a black
telephone in the snow, then a spotted orchid.
What I am showing you is the exploded view.

Cracked bird bath in the snow. Fallen tree, monograph
by a noted dendrologist. His children, heirs to his
headaches, will remember how he squinted at the page,
his papers thawing, in spring, to the contours of bark.

POPPY

Poppy that my heart was, sullen
mouth agape and buzzing in
the upper cavity of resonance

Poppy that my heart was, tissue-thin
petals a-droop, such doggerel
Demeter's narcosis for whosit

lost one doesn't sleep here,
she can't, somnia is a fall
slow enough to float, Poppy

had a heart made of paper and
tulle loops her mother sewed
to keep her wound up close

remember that my heart was
so inscribed on gravestone whilst
you, Canker Flower, did stray

remember, your mother was
a singer who sang herself
to sleep, she stitched you

your heart was hers, was
sonorant O of soprano
you, Poppy, were tethered

to the hum that hovered
there, inside her, you
Poppy, did kick.

FOLK SONG

Since they detangled the wires under my hair
and took out the bad parts, not even the bending
of light saddens me. I see a family glisten on the bay
in a white sailboat and perch awhile, invisible,
eavesdropping on their inner peace. A Bluefin tuna
blurs by, an immense iridescence with an underbite.
My mouth is wired to a trigger point on the sole
of my right foot. Press it and I say the funniest things.
Hiss-hiss go the dog-faced snakes in the vault, here kitty-kitty
goes the little engine that could. When I say she snapped,
I mean she danced like a suspension bridge
in an earthquake, fell into the strait, felt her neck give,
was left beheaded in a beaded dress with shoulder pads
and a stain. What does it mean when a chain store flies
its logoed flag at half-mast? He shook his fist
and laughed at me. I regained consciousness.
Even air has its blackouts. Think of the hundred-year
infestation, the sky a densely pixelated net of buzz.
Spores travel faster than I can sing. The scanner mistakes
a throat singer for a bomb. The singer stabs
himself in the heart. The scanner jumps off a bridge.
Toot-toot goes the little kid with his arm, hoping
the long-haul trucker will oblige. On the stereo,
a Bulgarian folk song about two shepherds
buried alive inside a mountain plays on.

EVENT

During the flood, I was robbed
in the church parking lot.
The monofilament bobbed
to the surface, but not before

I saw myself facedown in the river.
Before we lost our phone chargers,
but after the excommunication.
We had not yet forgotten

what it felt like to be cast out
for something we knew we had done.
I wanted to be left alone to wait
for the streetlamps to come on

before a palsied claw gripped
the shifter and beauty rolled down
the window of her midsized sedan
and spat at incoming traffic,

before you woke up with a sad hunch
before you woke up parched
with a bruised knuckle and a limp
and metallic discs of colored light

bursting in the corners of your eyes
like sequins on a heaving bust.
You used to think those lights
were signal mirrors flashed

by angels until you learned
they were just protein particles
suspended in the vitreous.
Your palms were sweating,

there was a smell in the air.

MY PEOPLE

My people are invisible. They are all around me, there is no one else. I wander
    these rooms, I walk on frozen ridges of mud and under
        the boughs of blighted hardwoods. Still, they whisper,
with all the leaves gone, you can really see the ground.

My people walked over mountains and buried children on the trail
    for a prophet who led them to a lake of salt.
Now they polish the temple in their secret clothes, for my people
    are luminous. Though I can't see them, they whisper, *you owe us.*

Forgive me, for I went to the woods hoping to catch leaves as they fell
    and woke up in the den with Grandma and Fox News.
        Maybe it's the clarity of a fever that I miss, or maybe
I really do believe. Maybe the hell I believe in has degrees.

THE IDEA OF

A Midwestern water park in winter is
like farting at the gym on a Stairmaster
or tripping in public only to glare at
the crack in the sidewalk that isn't there,
like using 'vestibule' in conversation
while standing at the lip of a hole
the size of eight city blocks. Trying to hail
a cab in West Lafayette, Indiana, is like tap water,
anywhere, like writing *Great!* on a piece
of paper, then underlining it twice,
which is sort of like betting on winning
a foot race in moon boots or building
a campfire on a beach with an incoming tide
or the way parties are lonely, like music.
Like quitting smoking for a few days
as you imagine the end of the movie
of your life, which is like the idea of
drowning that you have just minutes
before burning yourself.

DUSTING

Fumbled around in the dark
with my feathers, did my best
to feel down the corners
to squat, to trace
the baseboard with my face
found another corner
swabbed as far as I could
reached the seam of
wall and ceiling, finally
felt my way to the light
it was filthy, there were
signs of me everywhere
footprints in the dust
chalk smears in the shape
of my hand, tracks from
my knees from where
I had been crawling—

ASSISTANT

My act requires a certain economy
of gesture, a singe of the blade
in the velocity of white gloves.
Pure metals are too soft. I know

an alloy with no melting point.
I have mastered a calliope of nicks,
my scars so precise they glow
in the spotlight. My assistant purrs

like a torch singer in her sheath
of mauve charmeuse. She pins a bloom
behind her ear and smiles for you
as I strap her to the wheel, snug against

the target: painted outline of her body.
Watch her spangles spark off motes
as the music swells and the wheel spins
and the room spins and my blade

misses, sibilant in the fine hairs of her nape.
Ladies and gentlemen, I give you
my beautiful assistant. My first trick.

MUSE THE DRUDGE

I, hackneyed beauty queen cut
with kitchen knife, whir, tilt off

spin fast, a heavy eddy, I am no
girl-wisp, nor clipped wingtip

nor treachery of baubles, nor branded
by word, nor shut up in a cave

no-body, no birdie, I leak, call me
Sheela-na-gig, Astarte, Dora, cheap

whiskey in cut-crystal, watch it your
earlobe's in my teeth, I blow shit up

heart-husk, wax drip, I lick you, there
now you're licked. I, twitchy harlot

I, muse the drudge, poison cup, slipknot
not precious, not spread, here, hold it

to your ear, hear me laughing.
I, kitten-heeled, do drop kick.

I, I, I, beget, taste, hang by threads
of smoke, I cloy, my mouth drips

venery, I weave my own shroud,
burn ink, and dare you, speak of me.

LIVES OF THE PROPHETS

To see the bottom
of the well and say
hello and hear

only echo. To wonder,
and to know.
    To hear an echo

and know what is
before it comes.
To see the bottom.

Not to wonder, to know
shadows limp across
    the wall, smells

drip off the ends
of their arms. Hello, well.
    Hello.

IN SOTTO VOCE

for how long the crimped remain

and grope in the simultaneity

a keepsake, a timbre, a means

we will drift in regardless

snagged in thick weeds

to be put down again, to be instant

and find a hand outstretched as if

wicks of the knuckles were

hastened by their disfiguring

note its bulbous phosphorescence

and the train cars, the people

I am forgetting the particulars

moving across a vast slick surface

through filmy curtains

to say yes of course, my hand

against the abrasions of the clock

now look at you, you are entire

I will tackle sensations with strange barbs

I will put cream on my lobes

and vast the warp of the record

half-white alloy of the usual prop

I, a tiny mark on your knee

slivered offering

the bottom was drenched

the bishop says you cannot

all that, and the faint promise of

those white deer

and the place where I was raised

spitting in the wrong direction

the last time I saw her

an osprey: the sign says pardon

so I was up to my shins in it

a harbinger of half-light

I left my body to look for

flew over the crude sky

pleated on the bias

the left hand descending, softly

WINDS YOU HEAR BEFORE YOU FEEL

sound like traffic on the interstate, open your mouth
and the smoke alarm cries wolf and everything
becomes a study in loss, just one more hotel soap
in a collection of hotel soaps. Search the cushions
for change and find the thread that tethers
you to your body taut, but anchored there.
Stare at it, fidget your scars, aren't they better
than grease marks? Aren't they something?
So put your nose in the corner and count
out enough time for it to end. Calm the alarm
with a dishrag, stop the scuttle of inanimates.
Clear the debris of your dinner and all the
dog-eared evidence. Be static as a turbine,
photographed. Be a tinge of bleach in the water.
Listen to the wind wail as it rips through scales
like an elbow scraped across keys.

SELF-PORTRAIT AS TONGUE

When the acupuncturist examines
the film on my tongue, I'm afraid
she'll see I'm prone to night sweats

and sobbing at the dolphin show.
I hate the way they're made to do
tricks for food as if they were simple

humans with fantasies of interspecies
friendship. The acupuncturist nods,
says I run hot in the head and torso.

Basically, my meridians are fucked.
In California, roses bloom in winter
and plaques announce their breeding

names like racehorses, Dark Lady,
Crimson Glory, then it's Moondance
for the win! In an ad for gin, a woman

in a leopard coat walks a ferret
on a leash—no, the woman is
on a leash, in a leotard, in an ad

for what, I don't know. Worrying
generates heat which shows up
as deep red at the tip of the tongue

the only muscle in the body
not covered by skin and therefore
very telling. A strange kind of stress,

waving my hands back and forth
in front of a touch-free dispenser
waiting for its sensor to sense me,

a strange kind of convenience,
to access at the tap of a fingertip
so much information without

the ability to understand it.
Cataract means flawed vision
but also waterfall, cascade.

Dolphins only seem to smile
as the trainer commands them
to jump so high they splash

the front row in what will be
their fifth show of the day.
They can think of the future,

but can they also choose not to?
The audience erupts in applause.
I stick out my tongue and say *ah.*

CROSSING

I do not name, nor do I whisper after dark.
      In not naming, I call out

in hopes of being called. I am the frame

of a frosted window smeared by hands,
      the window of a night ferry. Dark water moves in me

and passengers stream sternward
      through the gnarls of my hair. I press my face

to the glass, cup my hands to form a seal and all
      reflection is gone. Relief—a darkness

so complete it diminishes water and sky to flatness,
      an absence against which

a few gulls drift backwards.

II

SORE SONG

Eros, you are so personless and difficult.
You hamstring us, string us up

and make us want to want only you: desire
dedicated to desire, the poison mandrake

roots and blooms and catches fire.
Your port barely conceals the everlasting

never enough. You are both ambulance
and chaser, stinger and the stung, swollen

welt and stinky balm. For you, we get lashed
to the mast. For you, we do the singing.

SORE SONG

All night I wait for you under the clothesline,
in the dew, the consecrated dew, in my new

wrap-dress with a pronounced décolletage
and scuffed shoes, in this same ordinary face.

All night horned chamois pad quietly behind
in the cypress grove and I find myself yawning

even as I feel you will not come, not even
when I bait you with mineral licks and fennel

and Bowflex, not even when I show you
the blueprints for my castle and point out

the countless scenic views. A trace of pollen
streaks your cheek. You lurk in an alcove

with a monkey wrench and leather driving gloves.
I clasp your picture to my throat and prisms

spawn rainbows in the humidity.
My tassels glitter delicately.

AN EVENING OF YES MUSIC

You roll over me in your office chair, poised
and manning your station in a ratty bathrobe,
not to be disturbed. I cover my head and try
to hear the crash of waves or the tremble

of a flute. With you at the podium, I crouch,
polish the chairs' lug nuts, crawl backward
down the aisle looking over my shoulder
with an eye on the exit sign as your voice

reaches out to thump every corner
and varnish the audience to a sheen.
There is nowhere I can go and not hear you.
I try the zippers on the sides of my face

but they are the cheapest zippers ever made.
I hereby dedicate them to you. I hereby
bequeath to you a cupboard full of bibelots.
Next, I'll suggest an evening of yes music,

light a kerosene lamp and put your hand
on my breast. Trust me, there are things
about me you don't want to understand.
I'm so rotten. Scrape me out and see

how I come alive in your hands.

ORIGAMI

There are windows we fly through,
and windows we fly into. We played
in the waves until a wave crashed

over us. What came next I don't know,
but you were there, and you said
that looking at me makes you forget

what I'm saying. Inside a file folder
labeled "Debts" are photos of men
I have committed to memory.

I can pinpoint the exact moment
I become boring, but only in retrospect.
A Luna Moth mauls a porch light

and across the world, someone files
bankruptcy. People get caught up
in causality, building entire careers.

The astronomer lives atop a dormant
volcano with his infrared telescope,
sifting for dust storms that may someday

form stars. So atmospheric turbulence
blurs his view, so what. Turbulence
makes stars shiver and wink.

SORE SONG

Meet me at the secret airport. You'll know me
by the spinner lure in my hair and it will feel like

the first time I saw you on the cover of a magazine
lying next to an empty bottle in some other

woman's kitchen. I could go home but for the glint
of your wristwatch in a room of antique automata,

your many fabulous contingencies, the *if* and *when*,
the *what now*—darling, how I miss the strangers

I used to know, their cozy odes and felted doublets,
their igloos and fronds, the reek of dove scat, and all

their histories rubbing up on me, the mere proximity
of their tattooed forearms! I miss the worthlessness

of minutes spent waiting for a cab, beep of a truck
backing in, a bad cover band warming up on the pier,

your face in a newspaper ad strewn across a bench,
plastic bottle caps and yogurt foils winnowed

and teased by wind until finally the band grinds out
the grittiest ballad of modern love in all its tattered

attenuations. And the chorus, that soaring chorus:
please come on to me, so I can get out of here.

SO FAR GONE

I don't know anything about the speed of sound
except that subsonic and supersonic sound like

garage rock and maybe something about waves,
the way sound changes over distance, marred

by a million echoes, scraped smooth as beach glass
through invisible interactions with space.

The most beautiful songs are the ones you can
barely hear because they are so far away, *so far*—

so gone, which is the sound of foghorns on
the Golden Gate intoning their own requiem

with each delayed two-tone as satellite-guided
GPS may soon eliminate the need for them.

I wonder what interval that is in music theory,
which I flunked freshman year. "Foghorns (Golden

Gate) with light traffic noise" is a sound effect
you can buy online and it's weird to hear it

at the bus stop on a morning with perfect
skies, everyone looking around to see

whose phone that is. We are lonely.
Even the foghorn itself is now automated,

a laser beam shot out to sea, a sensor
that talks to a computer, like most people

the sound of the foghorn is determined
by the landscape through which it must travel,

often overwhelming in extreme close-up
though dear when heard from far away.

SORE SONG

In a quick smear before full focus, the eye
misreads what it wants to see, whole cities

hopefully elided, words reversed, double-
negatives parsed and reparsed 'til they thrum

taut as piano wire. So too the ear hears what it needs
or what it fears, and every letter turns love letter,

whether scrawled in sidewalk chalk or blinking
pixels on a reader-board gone berserk, *please*

help, hungry in Sharpie on cardboard or a slick
promo subject line, *It's not too late!* or this safety

orange classic flipped in haste: *sorry, we're closed.*
I strain to hear you, listen so hard my eyes cross,

but in your honeyed mumble everything sounds like
please come for me, or *don't comfort me.*

The line crackles, consonants lost in wind and miles
of wireless wires. I'm sorry, did you say *mistake?*

I could have sworn I heard my name.

LONGEST SONG

His fingers plinked broke
strings on the bridge, lit
brush fires in an elbow crease

shhh, it was like being alone
how come notes hung so
heavy in his hand that he picked

up the pieces of his face, hit
a low hiss of rain and carved—
mutter-mutter—a pang

rubbed into the unbearable
twoness of three, I mean
of one, how come broke

stereo breaks into mono
with the low amp hiss of
a house built of matchsticks

and lit, why does melody so
scraped break how his face did
when a door slammed and

the edges began to water—
mutter-mutter—in memory
a pang, rings with no fingers

loneliest thing I ever heard
was a song long as a splintered
prime number, it just hung there

like smoke, threading

SORE SONG

I woke from a dream about rationing and meat
rotting in a storage locker and knew I was lonely.

All I wanted was to kiss on a sparse, late train, dark
platforms, flickering, nothing fancy, just to unravel.

So I mistook the employee for a mannequin.
Sometimes I still mistake statues for men

who remember me. I miss your slanted heart.
Please send a graph of its irregularities, some proof

you haven't forgotten how your fingers felt
in my mouth, the way you hooked into me.

Maybe you were just some metal flashing in the sun,
but I don't want to drive back to the subdivision

blubbering like a radio cliché, all the days blank
panels waiting to be narrated, some echo in a tunnel,

some junk to delete. Let me show you how it feels
to feel we deserve anything like love.

MEMORY IS A BULL MARKET

How embarrassing—an ABBA song
looping in my head and the vague sense
I'm being tailed by a squirrel in a red
jumpsuit waterskiing behind a remote-
controlled boat at an auto show.
If I were more than all I've left behind,
I'd have a phantom heart murmur
and perfect skin and not a twinge
at the omission of some polite gesture,
that sharp whiff of yesterday's fried fish,
some moment I neglected in which
something crucial was hidden,
the plastic egg we never found
that fades from teal to a hue much closer
to the color of the real. Once again,
the song requeues and rescues, syrupy treble,
then that eponymous chorus, so shrill
and unforgettable. I could tell you lies
so beautiful you'd be sobbing
into your napkin in no time, and what
I couldn't make up, I'd remember.

LET'S PRETEND

Let's pretend this is the best song ever
crank it up and pretend we're tourists
in shorts with maps and in love

let's pretend that kiss was an accident
blame it on boozy excitement,
let's pretend we're Italian and stroll

la passeggiata on the Via del Corso,
let's pretend my cousin in Idaho
doesn't have guns plural, pretend

we're in labor and push, pretend
the alert wasn't amber and the lost
child was found safe and alive

hiding under her bed, pretending
let's pretend we're rich and thin
slouch laconically on a balcony

let's pretend our ears don't burn
nod yes with a mouthful of rare beef
dab tears of contentment, pretend

we are a happy family of four
and it's bath time, then bedtime
read a story about ourselves

as rabbits and squirrels who live
in thatched-roof cottages with
secret passageways, let's pretend

our secrets make us interesting
let's pretend we don't remember
let's pretend we remember everything

what's that smell? It wasn't us
the error module does not recognize
the error, let's pretend we are

who we say we are, that we wave
at mayors in parades and always
call back our moms, this works best

when we're unbearably sad
this isn't fun anymore
so what, pretend that it is

pretend that pretending
is different than lying and we
don't see a black Mercedes

circling the block and this
waterfall is not powered
by electricity, we are not

powered by electricity
this dead-end is not
the real-deal end.

GRIMACE

Regret does not descend in a cinematic miasma.
It hits like nausea, creaks back and forth
on a limited axis like one of those vaguely
eggplant-shaped metal cages you used to see
in fast-food playgrounds across America.
Meanwhile, the sky unfurls its violent ribbons
and karate kids spar on the green. I am driving
or rinsing a dish, or picking zucchini, whatever
it is I do now that I've outlived my misspent youth,
confused by the hair-trigger pairing of regret
and nostalgia, ouroboros of endings that beget
other endings, memory like a waterwheel
we're tied to, half-drowned and just trying
to make it around one more time.
Grimace, I embrace you from the inside.
The place is empty, let me stay awhile.

MIDSUMMER SINGALONG

We carried the canoe on our shoulders to a deep green
        mountain lake where the reflection of trees seemed
more vivid than the trees, glided across to a star-shaped rock,
        shed our layers, dove in, and though I'm not sure
the lake was real, I remember the swimming was beautiful.

Now a few lemons on the kitchen table, chipped teacup
        of bluish milk, stack of empty jewel cases, and a cold
wind blows through the single-pane window bleared with salt
        and interminable fog. Dear you, this isn't the story we told.
I was holding out for a teary slo-mo reunion at the Laundromat,

Me in a scant sundress, cicadas in my hair, you with a compass,
        in loafers and no socks, the whole gang grapevining
behind us in unison on checkered linoleum, everyone pretending
        to fall in love until we were pretty sure of it. If we must
forget, let the forgetting be perfect. The days grow shorter.

Soon a team will arrive to inspect our memories for error
        and the great data scrub will begin. Idling in traffic,
blasting a power ballad laced with static, you'll lean
        your forehead against the window and not think of me
when you see someone walk away in your reflected face.

ANTHEM

Every pop song is just another song
about California, the waves, yeah
the waves, kids in the boom-boom
room shaking ass in the smoke

machine smoke like they're dancing
in a gold cage, dudes singing along
bobbing their heads in midlife
crisis cars like they're not alone

in traffic, blonde girls vogueing
a looping dumbshow on Vine
for faraway boys with lathery
torsos, and the chorus goes

hi-lo blow-pop shuga-shuga shake—
every club song is lonely, is a song
about longing generally, every
song about California dreaming

is sad the way a Solo cup rolling
on its side under a palm tree is,
and neon blinking *Palms Read Here*
is just another way to say take me

to the bridge, let that big 4/4 beat
build to the bridge, surge of blood
away from the brain, beats like boxes
where we can have all the feelings,

dance so close to the speaker the bass
hurts our kidneys, be predictable as
let's stay for just one more, anonymous
as bodies on the floor.

SORE SONG

Hey you, tune in that sonar. Come on down
with your fanged kiss, bow rosined and held aloft,

ascot crooked, but rakishly so. How I've missed
scanning the horizon for you, wary of parallax—

decadent, the way it screws with the curves.
I need your thumbprint on me in glitter or in ash.

I looked for you in bulk bins of star anise,
in the creases of bus seats, in strange twangs

and interstate clovers, mistook you for other
pangs and baubles, and lay awhile panting

in your shadow, laid wait in stairwells
and in the body's many clefts, whispered

for you, parched, once thought I saw you
through a guitar pick's tortoiseshell, once

caught a glimpse of the hem of your robe.
I sensed you with my high-powered sensor.

I orbited you, I probed. And now I see your
massive eye blink against the bars of the cage

as my vessel pulls closer, risking burn-up for data.

III

PASSENGERS

Sashimi-grade and days old, we were slashed

like prices for the card-carrying member.

Now we operate mostly with the safety on.

Told to handle it, so we handle it.

Crickets burn in their customary fervor,

but transposed up a key and sharper. We resist the urge

to sand it down so smooth we sand right through it.

Solicitors queue up and there's nobody home to hide from them.

The blinking clock bespeaks the digital redness we are feeling.

In the marginalia, a child holds your hand and counts to three

before jumping into the sidewalk chalk drawing.

Our connection was running so slow we had to think

between pages loading.

Dogs circled, pointy as sharks.

It was autumn, and porch rails ensnared in poison oak turned glamorous.

We, too, used to work in shifts.

We want something scalable, less whirling.

The meds keep us even, but we miss desire.

The dream was so bad it woke me.

I was holding myself.

Like the stabbing realization of loss, anticipated.

Rip the two-by, grease the jigsaw.

All night, jets pace the sky.

Where are they going.

DO NOT LEAVE THIS BOX

Do not leave this box in heat and sunlight.
It might rot. It might already be rotten.

Still, cherry trees blossom and grow heavy,
and in the bog that stretches from the shadow

of the superstore, a Sandhill crane folds
minnows in its beak. Stiff-legged, a woman

in the stockroom unbinds the plastic-bound
boxes from pallets that arrive on trucks,

twenty tons per container, one of many
the cranes stack stories high on the ship

loaded to heavy displacement in Shanghai
to course across shipping lines at speeds of

over twenty knots. Be careful with this box.
Most likely it has crossed the ocean more

than twice, first as product, then as fiber bought
in tonnage and recycled for remanufacture

as corrugated board, then expertly assembled
in the Zhejiang Province by a young woman

who pressed its corners with aching hands.
Under her mattress she's hidden a set of nested

ornamental boxes. On the lid of the smallest
is a woodcut of a crane, for luck.

OSTINATO

The new company logo is a torch inside an obelisk
inside a five-pointed star inside a sixteen-sided die
against a backdrop of blazing sunlight. It took years
of focus groups, an in-house creative team collecting

only the smoothest, flattest stones from the banks
of the minor tributaries of each river beloved by
our target demographic, research into their concentric
patterns of worship, the lives of their saints, the miracle

of the giant tropical lake found on Saturn's Titan Moon
so like that box of tissues in the conference room
that never empties in the face of organizational betrayal.
At the quarterly meeting of shareholders, the chief officers

unveiled several new prayers for the test markets: nothing
is impossible—it is your responsibility to make it so,
let us search for management in a stargazing field, let us
sustain new synergies among alleged victims, give us

this day our daily sales cloud. You are the blue arrow
pointing down to a box half-shaded in gray on the flowchart.
Here is your cubicle, your stapler. Burt is your team leader
though this period of consolidation. He developed

an upgrade that renders the old product obsolete
for which he received a fat raise and the right to keep
his desk utterly bare. The shareholders believe
he is an oracle, that he peers into that empty, elegant

veneer, his mind a crescendo underlying a persistent
musical pattern, the end of desire itself, one killer app
for the one Oregonian suffering sunset's vague lilac,
one step towards the eradication of mediocrity among

normal children. Your team emblem is a kitten,
your alibi is that you never watched a whole episode.
When the supervisor asks how the product changed
your life personally, be vague, say you dream less

of free diving with dolphins in bloody water and more
about your fear of elections. As you peruse the directory,
try not to notice how many names have been crossed out.
Be grateful for the key card hanging around your neck.

Dear coworkers, let's hold a séance in the parking garage,
erase all the voicemail in the world, paint zeroes on our faces
with printer ink, insist we are as impeccable as executive
letterhead in ivory, as cheerful as we appear to be

in the video of the company party, more efficient than
crepuscular rays, worthy of outlasting the outsource,
and lucky enough not to know just how narrowly
we escaped the meandering, photochemical haze.

I-BEAM

We stand on the overpass with the wind at our backs.

Told to please hold, so we hold.

We have been groomed for this. We are an elite squad.

It's like there's a whole world down there under the surface.

The heart's missile misfires.

A fishhook in the eye and it's ours for the taking.

I am looking at a photograph of a bridge where a man was beaten.

Everyone has a place they won't talk about.

It's stop-and-go from I-to-I and the drivers are rubbernecked.

There are judgments, and there are precedents.

Once a week, they blow the leaves to the curb.

Once a week, the city removes them with a vacuum truck.

Two blocks south, the river runs backward

incanting satanic messages.

Vigil is relative, vigilance is candlelit.

Our window is near the wing. We never sit on the aisle.

Russet foliage turns and drops as though hot.

White worm in the compost, grace under hire.

The epiphany is a feat of optics

like the size of my hand underwater.

You think what you hear is a song.

Turns out it's just someone dusting the keys.

ELEGY

Autumn leaves don't fall. The trees eject their dead
to survive the winter, the gaunt steer mounts the cow
in a brown field, a hearse slows all the same
for a deer or a skunk, and rake tines still break
the surface of the ground like the justified howls
of teething babies that pierce the tabernacle
or the chanting of priests as they flash their ancient
gang signals. Promise me that when the old man dies,
somebody will still feed the Jays.

Gone the iridescence of cellophane caught in a branch,
gone the wound up youths with their jejune and wiry follicles,
gone the jaunt and the feathery knuckles of barnacles,
gone the barnacles, for they have no heart, only a sinus
close to the esophagus, gone the coils of tobacco curing
like tangled red wigs from the barn rafters and the hungry
foals asleep at dawn, gone the edema and the groan,
and the diapered man cut down like a stand of Shagbark hickory,
his voice hauled out of him, a cord of stolen firewood
that burned before anyone remembered it was split.

Through the cataract of my sunglasses' cracked lens,
I see what the freight train sees: the ass-ends
of slumped houses, dogs dragging lengths of swing set chain,
Jays pricking bush berries with a brusque possessiveness.
How mean they are, I mean, how brave
to ignore the whiney flight patterns of small planes
and the busts of parking meters and all these other

signs of interference. Promise me that when this bouquet shrivels, you will kick it off his grave.

NATURE

Hers is a callousness we wish for in odd moments of the night.
She is a steering wheel in the desert, dark accelerator
in the database, young enough to remember lasers
yet empty enough to hold all of us. She rubs vaporous
ointment on our balsa chests and gives us just enough
time to forget what we have wasted. So we worship

her charismatic megaparticles with sweet miscalculations,
imagine her ear as canticle, her eyelash as necklace.
When she brandishes her prosthesis, hydrogen blooms
its elephantiasis. Our nametags say we are sympathetic,
a lazy cross-breeze cools the backs of our legs, and still
this minivan with the flat-black side-panel has no muffler.

What could the maimed want from us? We, who made
piano wire, we who were born on the eve of appetite,
on the wings of Saturday night, and will pay for it
with blue-tongue Slurpees and plastic leis. What a racket
she makes. Imagine her cerebellum as a flea circus
and Ruby-throated hummingbirds halt their migration,

imagine sixteen different possible futures for wildfires,
her mouth as a literal souvenir, and she mutates
the gross mammalian heart, comes unhinged, mascara
ruining her cheeks as she screams *don't you walk
away from me, you bastard*, and flings her red shoe,
narrowly missing the back of some guy's head.

VANTAGE

It begins with a prick at the ankle.
The maple tree buds false in the bare copse.
Bodies roll out of cargo bays wrapped in flags.
Nothing could prepare us for this.

There is a curvature. We shrink to depict
distance. A dead finch wings by in the dirt
by the grace of maggots' invisible strings.
When does refraction turn myopic?

When it impairs normal functioning.
Who determines that? We do.
Liberally, we apply the poultice as fireflies
blip in the periphery like dizzy stars

in brief moments of oxygen deprivation.
The flatter the painting, the more we marvel.
We can't help it, it reminds us of children
who draw what they don't understand.

Far from the vanishing point, they grow.
By what means? I don't know,
but I've been walking for days.

WAYMARK

I lost my keys in a meadow and stumbled along the castle's
dank passageway only to emerge squinting before a green screen.
You touch a whorl of matted grass where a deer lay and call it
child's hair damp with fever, now cool to the touch with dew.
Quiet, now. Bells in the square ring at strange intervals
and no shadows lengthen. In another country, this medicine

is called *Moment* and it is very expensive. Visitors are asked
to remove their shoes before entering. The master waved
from the carport and midges swarmed the motion-sensor light
as we backed down the driveway. Our feelings oscillated
like glass cylinders as we recalled his hands on our heads,
the scratch of his beard, faraway sound of sawing, and we knew

it was time to go. Everyone at the same time across time zones
thinks the word *wind rose* and a wind rose appears in all
those places at once, avatar of itself, perfect duplicate
yet somehow irreducible. What difference does it make,
where I am. Walking the length of a soccer field twice-
bracketed with goals: regulation size, and inside, the child's

cupped like hands in larger hands, the whole field circled
by a track of red clay flooded at one end and therefore
reflective of the sky. Visitors are asked to obtain coordinates
for each target location. A vast parking lot shimmers
in late Midwestern summer, jangle of shopping carts, loose
cymbal crash of one cart collapsing into a chute of carts,

while the Italian girl with purple spiked hair sings along
to the Talking Heads in beautiful, slanted English and I'm lost
in the foothills of the Cascade Mountains, now running
around a red track, now reclining on a velvet cushion
on the floor of a villa covered in frescoes depicting itself
and the surrounding countryside. Note the symmetrical

plantings, tidy wicks of cypress. Not only is this typical
of the region, it's the ideal that defines the type, its history
documented in thousands of files abandoned in a vault.
In the hospital waiting room, a woman in white tennis shoes
also sits very still, not bothering to look at the *Redbook*
in her lap or the little boy swinging and swinging his legs,

surge of the sea of the brain, then a dark plasma screen.
You don't know where this has been. I'm trying to explicate
the serene imbalance of the structure. Note the way its wings
flank the center. In the courtyard, a sundial's gnomon casts
the hour and the sign of the zodiac with points that fall
on the circumference of an ellipse. The former end of the world

is a windswept, wedge-shaped promontory at the very most
southwestern tip of Portugal. Here, the navigator prince foresaw
his empire opening oceans, ships returning with gold, ivory, slaves.
Creating negative space around the body allows for cooling
properties in the swelter. Flashes, though the pictograph
clearly depicts a crossed-out camera. Lovers might consider

getting a room at the Aurora Borealis Motor Inn in Michigan.
See a Samsonite suitcase at the bottom of the pool. A polka-dotted
blouse floats to the surface and you think of a hole the size
of another hole you saw the last time someone said *promontory*.

In fair weather, it is pleasant to sit anywhere along cliff tops,
but now it's raining in the presbytery, it's hailing in the apse,

and in the fresco above the door to the sacristy is a self-portrait
of the artist as lamb. In his bedroom, an awkward teenager
plays the theme from *Cheers* on his synthesizer while his stepdad
tills the backyard for stones. In the colonnade, you may notice
the influence of a certain master in the way the Madonna eyes
her charge. Though traces of destruction are evident, we fail

to recognize the familiar city. Search by country, search by region,
stand at the apex of a curve of a bridge. In the evenings, a change
of guard. Here, the master furrows his brow. Note the pattern
of his labored breathing, his dilated pupils. If you see the imperfect
circle he makes when he touches his thumb to his finger, you might
suspect a falsification of perspective and know that you've arrived.

FILL THIS BOX WITH FLAMES

Fill this box with flames
and cut grass cordoned
in a ring of hiss, give it
a window sash and flounce,

fingerspell your name
in the fog of breath against
its pane. If it asks to be
laminated in transparency,

fill it with iodine and Worcestershire,
deface it with magic marker,
for boxes like these cannot be
penciled in, nor foiled by

ink blot, though they may
ask you to sing a few bars,
remember that we are not
really ourselves, but perfect

copies of a long-lost original,
a revolutionary system
so gentle it removes the stone
without bruising the fruit,

repairs the gaping hole
in the fuselage without
disturbing the survivors,
so fill this box with flames

or static blips, but be gentle.
Since the crash, none of us
have been the same.

BOBBY READS CHEKHOV

We think we know, but still we look it up
on our phones only to discover a giant sea serpent
has just been found off the coast! Personally,
I never doubted the accounts of all those sailors
of antiquity, though months at sea and regular
bouts of scurvy must occasionally distort
one's sense of proportion. Do we really need
scientists to prove that listening to sad music
leads to catharsis, or that dogs feel shame?
As Bobby reads, a wedge of his brain glows
slime-green like that old Simon Says game.
Evidently metaphors arouse the sensory cortex.
Sexy. Some days, my yard becomes a metaphor
for everything I do wrong: moldy dog shit,
stray butts, a shrub's yellowed leaves.
They say if you're sad, you haven't been
smiling enough. Want to make better decisions?
Eat more cheese. Perception is reality,
my horrible boss used to say when I'd try
to explain anything she couldn't see,
though maybe she was right. Can we know
reality any other way? The painter saw
purple in the trees, so he painted them purple.
Leaving the gallery, we see purple everywhere.
Studies have shown meditation produces
brain waves akin to coma. Is that so,
you say, fingering your tiny screen.

THE BRAIN MAY DISASSEMBLE ITSELF IN SLEEP

Every night, neural connections unravel a little
as your mind edits itself and resets, making way
for recently formed memories to replay
and become more sharply etched. You dream
of a lanky lawyer in a flawless dress shirt
who smells faintly of hotel lobby and of ham,
not to mention the dream about teeth. Julia says
teeth mean control, but you're pretty sure
they mean death. Either way, it's not good
to dream about your mother in the tall, wet grass,
her arms folded as if to say, what are you waiting for?
And when Julia appears in tattered lace with
a green ribbon around her wrist and tells you
her terrible secret, you are happy because
she finally told you what you already knew.
It is not enough to say we are transparent things.
The captain cracks his knuckles over the intercom.
The sun sets in the cracks of a haggard, snowy peak
while wildfires in the West rage against the blowing dust.
Every September, the arctic ground squirrel
burrows beneath the tundra to curl up in a nest
of lichen and caribou hair. Its heart slows,
its lungs slow, its temperature dips below freezing
and electrical signals vanish in many areas of its brain,
but don't worry. Soon it will awaken and return
to the surface of the earth, hungry and eager
to mate, just as you will wake up with creases
on your face on a plane still circling airspace,

waiting for permission to land, just in time
to see clouds unraveling magenta, your brain
nicely blank but for vague pulses of light.

POINTILLIST

Come closer. The pupil constricts, striating
the surface of a leaf stuck to the stem
of a bloom: camellia. To appreciate
the many beautiful varieties, one must see
more than one, over time, or in thumbnails
twelve to a page, propagating in overlapping
aggregates, like petals. From here, I can see
state lines that trace the feet of mountains
and the palimpsests of riverbeds,
and others so straight they split grass blades.
Division is a matter of scale, just look at a map.
Now squint: use brown in case the paper's
bleached fiber is not enough to indicate,
when properly bordered, the face.
And now, to draw the eye: a single dot.

DESIRE LINES

Desire lines etched in the ground record the ways
    we wish constructed paths would take us,
grassy shortcuts, diagonals across fields
    like check marks or cross-outs, ruts

where a corner has been rounded off, dirt tracks
    running parallel with streets that express
where a sidewalk ought to be. They speak
    of our rush when the given way is circuitous

or has gaps, showing us what is easy or most safe.
    How many footsteps does it take
to make a trail that then attracts further use,
    until the desired way becomes its own way?

Travelers in the Botswana bush who ask if they
    are on the right road are told *it is a road,*
but it is not the road. In Detroit's urban prairie,
    pheasants nest in city blocks, a man

hunts raccoon to sell as food, and the footpaths
    that crisscross vacant lots tell us something
is missing, or turning over again. The purest desire
    lines appear in deep snow.

An aerial photograph of winter, rural Colorado:
    black lines spider and spread where the herd
dispersed, then a thickening, dark mass of tracks,
    cattle gathering around what must be

feeding troughs, the way a hunter knows
        all game trails lead inevitably to water.
A doe bends to drink from a creek, pauses
        ears alert, nose quivering in a shifting wind.

So too your last movements may be known,
        a vortex stirred up by a jet's wingtips,
invisible path lines recording fluid particles
        in the flow, vapor trails that endure

at high altitudes long after the jet is gone,
        damp exhaust spewing traces of water
and ice into already saturated air. In the book
        of cloud studies, halo clouds appear

above pitched rooftops in stark black and white,
        looking eerily like contrails, though
the photographs were taken years before
        the first jet flew. The author complains

the landscape paintings of his day are *disfigured*
        by impossible skies with vague, shapeless clouds,
as untrue to nature as it would be possible
        to make them. He wants us to see clouds

as they really are, or as they were, since jets
        have since altered them. An interactive map
reveals twenty-four hours of sped-up flight activity,
        blue lines tracing every flight path

in the world, myriad contrails like meteor showers
        on repeat or missiles lobbed in an arcade game
before the flight simulator screen racing with clouds
        flashes *GAME OVER*. Out of quarters,

you follow a path worn into the carpet's geometric
        pattern that points not the way out, but a way
to keep circling when you don't want to
        or don't yet know how to stop.

THE GREEN ROSE UP

It didn't matter that we wore our silver suits.
Cities welled up and were overwhelmed.
The green kept rising until we waded in algae
and at night a phosphorescent bloom
lit the pathways our limbs had traveled
and pocked the surface of the water with sparks.
Inland, sycamores gnarled towards the bank.
We banged on the doors of the institution,
but nobody heard us. We tipped our hats
then crumpled them in our hands
and did a little soft-shoe without knowing
what we were asking for. The green rose up
and we couldn't see past it. Vines covered
the brick debris, a pheasant nested
in the high grass of the razed block and
all around us was condemnation and vacancy.
So, we left the city, we left our clothes.
We lined up at the agency and spoke
only of our strengths and not of the law
that keeps us upright in the Rotor ride,
ironed to a curve. When we say we want
to live in the moment, what we mean is
we want not to want an impossible future.
To be conscious of every breath
is to be unable to think of anything else,
which is to say, happier.

SELF-PORTRAIT AS ELEGY

What an act of denial, hurtling through space
in so much steel and plastic like it's a video game.
As I cross the iconic bridge, I try not to think

about the speed at which the body of Weldon Kees
hit the riptide-bristled water when he was younger
than I am now. His body was never found,

unlike Amy's, who we called Knife Girl
after the incident with the switchblade and cake.
So many years sober, then one slip, she's dead.

I like to imagine I'm getting smarter now
that I know things like the heart is mostly water,
but I still get carded buying cigarettes after yoga.

I know, I'm trying. At night, my neighborhood
is very quiet but for the occasional lunatic
setting fire to a trashcan and a pack of girls

whose hyperbolic gestures of inebriated
affection I watch from my window.
Will my body gnarl and yellow? Silly question.

In a parallel universe, my friend Finn is still
seventeen, painting his fingernails blue
and swaying as Nico sings *I'll be your mirror*

and not also gone this year. That was years ago.
I reached that point in the poem and didn't
know how to finish it. What an act, hurtling

through space. Today, Facebook tells me
to wish Amy a happy birthday, so I go
to her page, now a virtual memorial,

scroll down, back in time, as better-place
sentiments give way to sadness, bargaining,
anger, then disbelief, grief blurred in reverse,

and here it is, the very last thing she wrote,
3 a.m., she can't sleep. She posts a photo
of a woman's mouth, a bullet in her teeth.

NOTES
AND ACKNOWLEDGMENTS

"Poppy" takes as its refrain a line from H. D.'s poem
"Phaedra."

"The Brain May Disassemble Itself in Sleep" takes its title
and inspiration from a May 2012 article in *Scientific
American*.

"Desire Lines" contains a quotation from the 1905 book
Cloud Studies by Arthur William Clayden.

My gratitude to the editors of the following journals and
anthologies where many of these poems first appeared,
sometimes in different versions: *Anti-; The Associative Press;
Best New Poets 2016; Blackbird; Boston Review; The
Cincinnati Review; Drunken Boat; Forklift; Ohio; Fourteen
Hills; Gulf Coast; Hayden's Ferry Review; Indiana Review; Jet
Fuel Review; jubilat; Juked; The Laurel Review; New
American Writing; New Ohio Review; Pebble Lake Review;
Red Light Lit; Remembering the Days That Breathed Pink: A
Collection of Women's Poems; Prose and Lyrics; Sixth Finch;
Southeast Review; Sprung Formal; Third Coast; The Turnip
Truck(s); Verse Daily;* and *West Branch*.

Some of these poems also appeared in a chapbook,
Flyover, published by Q Avenue Press. Other poems
appeared in the chapbook *Sore Songs*, published by Dancing
Girl Press. I am grateful to those editors.

Gratitude also goes to the Fine Arts Work Center in
Provincetown, the Prague Summer Program, the University
of Iowa Writers' Workshop, and the Vermont Studio Center

for giving me the time and support I needed to write many of these poems.

Thank you to Jericho Brown and everyone at the University of Utah Press. Thank you to Jocelyn Casey-Whiteman, Lauren Haldeman, Kristin Hatch, Patricia Henley, Mark Levine, Simone Muench, Srikanth Reddy, Lauren Shapiro, Luke Sykora, and Ryan Walsh for your encouragement, and for reading and commenting on these poems at various stages.